LONDON
AS IT WAS

A PICTURE POSTCARD VIEW

Araf Chohan

DestinWorld
publishing

About the Author

Araf Chohan, although born and bred in Middlesbrough, Yorkshire, lived and worked in London for over 35 years and has a deep affection and great love for his former home. Living in the Hanwell and West Ealing areas of London when based at Heathrow as long-haul cabin crew for British Airways, Araf became addicted to the "London Life" and his love of history and architecture were fully indulged, in this his favourite city.

Araf has been collecting Victorian and Edwardian picture postcards since he was 14. Now 65, he has always had a particularly close relationship with his London postcard collection as the very first card he ever bought was in Portobello Market in 1967, and from then on was hooked. Over the years his London collection alone has grown to be over 10,000 cards of the city and its suburbs.

Ever Since his first solo visit 1966, Araf fell in love with London and has never wavered in this. Having travelled extensively (circumnavigating the globe for over 2 years in 1975-6) well before joining British Airways, Araf has always maintained that no city in the world comes as close to his heart as his former and second "home town" - London. Araf has visited many of the world's greatest cities on his many travels but London has been, still is and always will be, his Favourite city in the World.

Dedication

This book is dedicated to all those Londoners from every corner of the globe who have ever been fortunate enough to have been born and bred and lived in London over its 2,000-year history. This London, this city of dreams and ambitions where anyone, from any place or background and from all over the world can fulfil their every wish and desire. My London, your London, our London, considered and acknowledged today as the world's global metropolis; London -the greatest city on our planet.

First published 2017

Destinworld Publishing Ltd
3 Fairfax Road
Middleton St George
Darlington, Co. Durham DL2 1HF
www.destinworld.com

British Library Cataloguing in Publication Data.
A catalogue record for this book is available from the British Library.

ISBN 978 0 9955307 4 4

CONTENTS

INTRODUCTION

LONDON, is my favourite big city in the world, as it is for many from around the globe. Although I was born and bred in Middlesbrough, a town in North Yorkshire some 240 miles away, London was my home for some 35 years, and always will be my spiritual 'home town'.

London today is renowned for it's cultural, educational, medical, financial, commercial and professional services. It is a Global player in the world of aviation, entertainment, fashion, the media, research and development, plus sport. London dominates in every field.

The municipal population of Greater London in mid-2016 was estimated at some 8,787,890, making London the largest of any city in the European Union and accounting for some 13.4% of the UK population. The city's metropolitan area is the most populous in the EU with 13,879,757 inhabitants. However, it is important to note that London was previously the world's most populous city from around 1831 to 1925.

London is the world's most-visited city as measured by international arrivals and has the world's largest city airport system measured by passenger traffic. London is also the world's leading investment destination, hosting more international retailers and ultra-high-net-worth individuals than any other city.

London's universities and colleges combine to form the largest concentration of higher education institutes in Europe and in 2012, London also became the first city in the world to have hosted the modern Summer Olympic Games three times. London is also home to no less than four World Heritage Sites making it the joint top city in the world, alongside Rome.

There are some eight million trees in London, making the world's largest urban forest and, with almost 40% open green space, it is joint third in the world with Rio de Janeiro and Hong Kong - all are surprises to most people as all three cities are considered to urban rather than green "jungles".

London has an incredibly diverse range of people and cultures from all around the world, making it one of the most multi-cultural global cities. There are more than 300 languages spoken in the Greater London region today. Therefore, London's firsts are numerous to say the least, and its influence is immense. It cannot be understated.

As well as being a world retail capital, a hub for technology, and not forgetting that it is one of the world›s top tourist destinations, we should be amazed at the facilities on offer in this modern 21st Century city which sits on a long, 2,000-year history and centuries of architectural gems.

London in short, is a world leader in so many fields to its inhabitants as well as people from all across the planet for whom it is number one city - the greatest city in the world.

Having amassed old postcards for just over 50 years, the images in this book have been collated entirely from my much collection. The Edwardian grandeur of London on show here depicts the London of yesteryear, the London of Empire, and the Imperial London of a world now long lost. It was a London that can be seen here via these wonderful picture postcards in all splendour.

Araf Chohan

LONDON LANDMARKS

The 17th Century St. Paul's Cathedral with Cleopatra's Needle (an Egyptian Obelisk from 1460 BC) and the Victorian Blackfriars Bridge's all combine here in this very pretty postcard from around 1903 to give a stylised overview of some of London's famous Landmarks.

A wonderful vista of two of the capital's best known landmarks - the Tower of London and Tower Bridge. The sheer scale of the fortress that is the Tower can be gauged by the two tiny figures standing by the outer walls that once surrounded the original moat.

Although built almost 800 hundred years apart these two great London landmarks sit together in a very harmonious ensemble.

This road here fronting the National Gallery went from east to west and is now fully pedestrianised and integrated into Trafalgar Square. This view from the turn of the last century seems sparse and not very busy, but this was far from actuality as it was a very congested thoroughfare and had to be paved over up to the north side of the Square in 2003.

Nevertheless, we can see a lovey contrast as an early motorcar is parked next to a Hansom cab - a scene that would be no more within a few years.

In the same general area but from a few years earlier, this postcard has three four-wheeler Hackney cabs and one Hansom all clustered up close to the main entrance to the National Gallery. St. Martin-in-the-Fields Church dominates the far end at the start of Charing Cross Rd.

L.438 LONDON. ST. MARTINS-IN-THE-FIELDS. — JUDGES LTD

This fine postcard shows a Number 80 motorbus waiting at its stop outside the National Gallery. St Martin-in-the-Fields Church, built in 1722-26, is of a neoclassical design, by James Gibbs. The church was the inspiration of countless churches in the original Thirteen Colonies and is still copied today all across North America.

The sweeping Admiralty Arch marks an imposing entrance between Trafalgar Square and The Mall, which leads onto Buckingham Palace. This very clear and sweeping panorama shows the Arch from its Trafalgar Square entrance, flanked by other grand Edwardian buildings. Once the home of the First Sea Lord and various government offices, it is currently being converted into a hotel, restaurant and four apartments.

The Admiralty Arch has become a landmark building in London and incorporates an archway providing road and pedestrian access between The Mall, and Trafalgar Square. It adjoins the Old Admiralty Building, hence the name. The building was commissioned by King Edward VII in memory of his mother Queen Victoria, although he did not live to see its completion in 1912. This marvellous vista shows the grandness of the Arch as viewed from The Mall.

Horse Guards is a large Grade I listed historical 18th Century building built in the Palladian style in London's Whitehall. Behind this is the Horse Guards Parade Ground. These wonderful images show the main Whitehall frontage built between 1850-53, where the Household Cavalry officers are mounted and on duty, and where tourists continually gather on a daily basis to be photographed next to the guards on duty, which has been going on for a long time, as seen in the picture below.

This grand Government building is on the corner of Whitehall and Great George Street and fronts on to Parliament Square. Built in two phases, the above scene is from soon after the first phase was completed in 1908. The building was extended and finished in 1913. Today it houses HM Revenue and Customs and has been refurbished and restored to reflect its former architectural glory.

A breathtakingly beautiful view looking over Downing Street (on the middle left) towards the towers of the Houses of Parliament and Westminster Abbey. The lovely green tree canopy on the right is St. James's Park with the dome of Central Hall looming on the horizon on the extreme right.

A view of the Palace of Westminster, better known as the Houses of Parliament, taken from the opposite bank of the River Thames. This is one of the great vistas of the world.

Seen here from the Lambeth side this astounding image without a doubt shows just how the Parliament buildings dominate the north bank of the Thames, and is more than worthy of its world heritage status.

In this hand-coloured early 1900s postcard shows Westminster Hall, which is over 900 years old and a rare survivor of the 1834 fire which burnt the old Westminster Palace down. Having been built between 1097 and 1099, the hall is the oldest building on the Parliamentary estate and has an astonishing hammer beam roof.

It is impossible to imagine the streets around Westminster being this quiet today. The buildings on the left of the scene have since been demolished, however the Westminster Scholars War Memorial, erected in 1861, still stands.

Situated on the corner where Green Park and Hyde Park meet is the Wellington Arch. Originally topped by a statue of the Duke of Wellington, it now features the four-horse chariot quadriga statue. The busy A4 roundabout encircles it today.

L 425. WESTMINSTER CATHEDRAL. - JUDGES' LTD.

Often overshadowed by the nearby Westminster Cathedral, the unique striped brick tower of Westminster Abbey stands proud over the surrounding buildings. The home of the Catholic Church in England and Wales, this large structure was completed in 1903 and is home to the Archbishop of Westminster.

The Hyde Park screen was designed by Decimus Burton and completed in 1828. From its beginning it became a much loved London landmark which to this today is revered. The Ionic columns and three arches were erected as a part of the grand approach to it, and as a corner entry to Hyde Park. The whole structure is often incorrectly called Hyde Park Gate, but that is the name of the nearby neighbourhood rather than the of the structure itself. This lovely postcard shows the structure in its Hyde Park setting with Apley House next to it.

Marble Arch is a 19th-century white marble faced triumphal arch and a very popular London landmark. Designed by John Nash in 1827 to be the grand entrance to the then Great Courtyard of Buckingham Palace, in 1851 it was relocated to Hyde Park and seen here in this fine photographic postcard. With the widening of Park Lane in the early 1960s, the Arch is today isolated on a very large and busy traffic island.

The church of St Clement Danes in the Strand was redesigned by Sir Christopher Wren in the 1680s, taking on the familiar architectural style of so many of his London churches. It was heavily bombed in World War II but restored in the 1950s. The tall tiered tower seen here and at nearby St. Bride's were often said to be the inspiration for the tall tiered wedding cakes which have become so popular since the Georgian period.

A stunning view of old London looking towards the towers and monumental dome of St. Paul's Cathedral. Other steeples and spires of Sir Christopher Wren's churches still dominate the London skyline as they did till the late 1960s when the first of London's skyscrapers were built.

This picture shows the still intact and clearly visible Victorian city, and is a wonderful visual record of the tightly packed medieval city that was to be destroyed by bombing in World War II and through subsequent redevelopments in the latter decades of the 20th Century.

The immense and monumentally grand British Museum located in the heart of Bloomsbury as seen in 1910. It is an example of Neo Classical architecture. With many extensions and additions the museum we see today is one of the largest in the world, housing vast collections collected and collated over the centuries. The central dome once housed the famous British Library reading room and the once surrounding open courtyard is now covered by a beautiful glass roof.

The Central Criminal Court of England and Wales, more commonly known as the Old Bailey, seen from the street on which it stands. The present building is a grand Edwardian building shown here soon after it's opening in 1907. With its huge central domed tower it dominates the narrow city street.

St Paul's Cathedral, London.

St Paul's Cathedral sits on Ludgate Hill at the highest point of the City of London and is a Grade I listed building. Seen here in 1909 is the Classical portico of the west front on its paired columns. The cathedral is one of the most famous and recognisable sights of London. Its dome has dominated the skyline for over 300 years, and at 365 ft high it was the tallest building in London from 1710 to 1967.

This coloured Edwardian postcard shows the Monument - a beautifully slender Doric Column which was built in 1671 to commemorate the Great Fire of London of 1666. Its flame top clearly shows the monument's raison d'être. The column's architect was the famous architect Sir Christopher Wren and the column is the tallest isolated stone column in the world.

THE MONUMENT

Established in 1694, the Bank of England is the second oldest central bank in operation in the world. The Threadneedle Street frontage seen in this evocative 1903 postcard image shows the lovely original John Soane building which was destroyed in the 1920s. Considered one of modern architecture's greatest losses, Soane's 1788 structure remained more or less untouched until it was demolished for the massive building we see today.

The coloured image above is of the third Royal Exchange building on the site that it still stands today. The image shows the Grand Portico of the main entrance which can be seen today almost unchanged today, minus the horse omnibus and the railings around the Duke of Wellington statue.

The Tower of London, officially Her Majesty's Royal Palace and Fortress of the Tower of London, is a historic castle and fortress located on the north bank of the River Thames. The very Victorian looking postcard is actually from 1908, showing the central 900-year-old Norman keep dominating the Tower precincts. Traitors Gate can be seen at bottom left, which once had direct access to the Tower complex from the River Thames.

The City of London School occupying a prominent position on the north bank of the Thames was opened in 1883 by Edward Prince of Wales. Established in 1834, the school was originally founded by an Act of Parliament and was for the poor children of the City of London. Today it is an independent day school for boys only, there being a separate sister school for girls, also in the City of London.

London - Cleopatra's Needle, Thames Embankment.

The obelisk commonly known as Cleopatra's Needle was brought to London in 1877 from Alexandria - the royal city of Cleopatra, and hence it's nickname. The painting-like coloured postcard shows the structure on its Embankment setting by the River Thames.

It was originally erected in the Egyptian city of Heliopolis on the orders of Thutmose III, thus making it the oldest man-made structure in London.

The beautiful and grand Somerset House seen here in its prominent position on the north bank of the River Thames, from a postcard of 1908. Built on the site of a Tudor palace, Somerset House is on a truly monumental scale. It was constructed in stages from the 18th to the 19th centuries and has wings surrounding a large square, stretching from The Strand to the River Thames.

Another view of the Neoclassical Somerset House. The postcard above shows the Waterloo Bridge facade, which is one of three major frontages of the building, alongside those on The Strand and the huge and impressive riverside.

The newly constructed Australia House seen here in 1918. It dominates and island site between The Strand and Aldwych. Built of Portland stone, many of the building's other materials were imported from Australia itself. The church of Mary-Le-Strand can be glimpsed on the left with its lovely slender spire piercing the London skyline.

Northumberland Avenue was laid out between 1876-78 and links Trafalgar Square with the River Thames. Although it is very small in length it mirrors the great boulevards of Paris, flanked by grand and beautiful Victorian buildings. This lovely 1905 postcard image shows Edwardian taxi cabs all lined up at the river end of the avenue.

The most northern stretch of Regent Street is seen here looking towards All Souls Church from a postcard sent in 1907. The Langham Hotel built between 1863 and 1865, the building seen here on the left, was at the time the largest and most modern hotel in London.

This 1909 postcard of the quaint Old Curiosity Shop of Dickens fame stands in Portsmouth Street in the heart of Westminster. This building, although dating back to the 16th Century, is believed to be the inspiration for Dickens novel of the same name.

The beautiful Burlington House in Mayfair seen here from a postcard of 1903. Once a private Palladian-style mansion, it is now the home to the Royal Academy of Arts. The busy scene above shows it's Piccadilly frontage with Hansom cabs lined up awaiting their next customers.

Ever since its opening by Queen Victoria in 1871, the Royal Albert Hall has been a premier music venue and a much loved and treasured London landmark. The distinctive circular style of the building makes it instantly recognisable, as does its scale and location opposite the Albert Memorial. Viewed here from just inside Hyde Park, the Hall has a magnificence which few buildings can match.

The Natural History Museum seen here in this wonderful view from a 1903 shows the famous Alfred Waterhouse Building which was opened in 1881.

The museum today is one of three in South Kensington grouped around Exhibition Road. However, the main frontage of the museum shown here dominates a whole city block along Cromwell Road.

The Oratory, South Kensington.

The Church of the Immaculate Heart of Mary in South Kensington is better known as the Brompton Oratory. It is a Grade II* listed structure with a strong history in music and teaching. It was consecrated in 1884 into the Roman Catholic church.

The now demolished Euston Arch was a monumental and much loved London landmark, now sadly just a distant memory for those still old enough to remember. The Arch was built in 1837 and was the original entrance to Euston Station. It was demolished when the station was rebuilt in the 1960s. The image above shows plenty of activity at the entrance to the station and shows the scale of the Arch.

Alexandra Palace is familiar to many who arrive or depart London by train from Kings Cross station, as it is clearly visible just north of the city from the train line. It is set in a prominent position in Alexandra Park and was built as an entertainment venue, rather than a residential palace, in 1873. Following a fire two years later it was rebuilt in its present form, and has been used for many purposes, including as a TV broadcast station, music and sports arena, and conference venue.

The Crystal Palace exhibition building was built in Hyde Park for the Great Exhibition of 1851. It was built entirely of cast iron and glass, and in 1854 relocated to Penge Common in South London, where it is seen in this picture. Although the giant structure was destroyed by a fire in 1936, the area was renamed Crystal Palace and is now home to a football team of the same name.

This is a rare photograph of the entrance to the Royal Hospital School at Greenwich. The beautiful training ship Fame can be seen centre stage with its tall masts dominating the scene. Two uniformed officers mingle with the crowds at the main entrance with young sailor cadets looking on.

Three different land-based training ships named Fame were built on this location for boys of the Greenwich Hospital School to train on, before the final example (seen here) was taken down in 1933.

In this very nice domestic looking view, what seems like a family of eight are looking at the clock on the wall of the Greenwich Observatory which is on the meridian line which gives its name to Greenwich Mean Time (GMT), setting the standard for time zones around the world.

This photograph is full of life, showing the Royal Greenwich Observatory where a large crowd has gathered to watch the Time Ball (visible atop the building) drop at precisely 1pm Greenwich Mean Time. Posh young men in boater hats and a beautiful early car with eager occupants all wait for the ceremony to begin.

PUBLIC SPACES

The Gordon (of Khartoum fame) Statue in Trafalgar Square in front of the National Gallery was a very popular spot to meet and relax to watch the world go by. The statue of General Charles George Gordon was erected on an 18-foot high pedestal between the fountains in 1888. It was removed in 1943 and re-sited on the Victoria Embankment, including its plinth, some ten years later where it stands to this day.

A wonderfully evocative view of Piccadilly Circus with one of the horse drawn buses which were a common sight in the city. Built in 1819 to connect then new Regent Street with Piccadilly, this is now a major London road junction as well as a popular tourist attraction with the much-loved statue of Eros

Ever since it's construction in 1819 Piccadilly Circus has been a major junction in the then newer part of the city. From quite early on in the 19th Century, Piccadilly Circus became a popular public space and a favourite spot for Londoners to gather. Later it became one of the main meeting places in city's night time scene, with its huge neon advertising signs making it famous all over the world. This wonderful view was photographed before the major reconstructions of Regent Street took place, which replaced all of the buildings shown here, other than those on the extreme right.

Another view of Piccadilly Circus in the heart of London. The building which is today covered in neon signage is on the left of this picture and Ripley's Believe It Or Not now occupies the London Pavilion building to its right. This very clear photograph from around 1914 is dominated by the new motorised London buses with little horse traffic now in evidence.

This is the original location of the Shaftesbury Memorial Fountain in the centre of Piccadilly Circus. It has since been moved to its south side. Named after Lord Shaftesbury, who was a prolific philanthropist and social reformer in London and responsible for many great works, the fountain was erected in 1892 to his memory. It depicts the Greek God Anteros and was given the name The Angel of Christian Charity, but is universally mistaken for his brother Eros.

Leicester Square is now a much-visited pedestrianised square in the West End of London. However, as seen in this early coloured postcard from 1903 the square was surrounded by busy roads on all four sides. Whitcomb Street is seen here, looking towards Charing Cross Road.

This companion postcard to the one above is a photographic card from the same viewpoint but taken some years later as can be seen by the early motor cars. All the buildings are exactly the same, with the famous Empire Theatre on the left.

In this wider view of Leicester Square the central gardens with fountains and trees can be clearly seen. The square was laid out as early as 1670 and is named after the contemporary Leicester House, itself named after Robert Sidney, 2nd Earl of Leicester.

The square was extensively refurbished and remodelled for the 2012 London Olympics and together with Piccadilly Circus and Trafalgar Square it is a very popular gathering place for Londoners and visitors alike, especially at night as it is at the centre of London's nightlife.

This fantastic photographic postcard from 1906 shows Trafalgar Square from an elevated position, with Nelsons column and the beautiful fountains from the 1840s giving the square a very impressive layout - as grand a public space as in any European city

The square's name commemorates the Battle of Trafalgar, a British naval victory in the Napoleonic Wars which took place on 21 October 1805 off the coast of Spain at Cape Trafalgar.

This incredible view of Trafalgar Square showing the grand building at the corner of Northumberland Avenue and The Strand. Also visible is the busy junction at the beginning of Whitehall. Nelson's Column, at just over 145 ft tall, looms over this fabulous scene and has done so since it's erection in November 1843. Trafalgar Square has been the premier gathering point in the city ever since its earliest days.

Now pedestrianised, the east side of Trafalgar Square is dominated by the 1832 National Gallery. The postcard above depicts a closer view of the lovely southern fountain (one of a pair) from the 1840s. The 1726 St. Martin-in-the-Fields Church located on the north-east corner of the Square dominates its corner site with its tall and splendid spire.

The National Gallery with St Martin-in-the-Fields are situated next to each other in this photographic view of Trafalgar Square.

St. Martin's is the church which is the inspiration for the design of thousands of small, traditionally-built churches all across America.

The junction shown here was then known as Charing Cross, but is now just part of Trafalgar Square, at the point where the statue of King Charles I overlooks Whitehall.

This marvellous scene of towers, turrets and spires overlooking Parliament Square towards the River Thames makes for an amazing vista. This wonderful collection of mostly Victorian Gothic architecture is a sight to behold. Under construction is and visible across the river just to the left of Big Ben is the former London County Council (later the Greater London Council) building.

The Queen Victoria Memorial is a marble monument to the long reigning monarch. Its location at the end of The Mall in London, and in front of Buckingham Palace, makes it a very visible and well-known London statue. Designed and executed by the sculptor Thomas Brock, it was unveiled on 16 May 1911, though it was not fully completed until 1924. The postcard view above shows the Memorial soon after it's completion but before the addition of the massive bronze figures with lions at the four corners of the monument.

Waterloo Place was created at the end of the 1820s as the final piece of the triumphal way that connected Regent's Park with Pall Mall. Construction, which included Regent Street as its centrepiece, started in 1810 to a winning design by the popular architect of Regency Britain, John Nash. This coloured postcard scene complete with carriages and a policeman give it a very Victorian feel, although it was taken many years after the death of Queen Victoria.

This wonderful photographic 1911 postcard view of Waterloo Place viewed from a high vantage point, looks towards the 112 ft tall granite column with a statue of Frederick, Duke of York and Albany overseeing the Mall. The white stucco Carlton House Terrace, designed by John Nash, can just be seen beyond the column, with Big Ben and the Houses of Parliament on the horizon.

Waterloo Place has many memorials and monuments, both large and small, to famous Britons. Amongst the more notable are those to the Crimean War of 1854-1856 seen in the image above, looking down Pall Mall. A separate statue to Florence Nightingale and many others are to be seen all around the square.

Another very famous Briton commemorated is Robert Falcon Scott, the explorer who made two expeditions to South Pole in 1912, after which he became known as Scott of the Antarctic.

One of the premier public spaces of London is Hyde Park Corner. It is seen here with Wellington Arch in its second position, as a gateway into the Green Park. Originally sited directly opposite Burton's Ionic Screen before it's removal to the entrance to Green Park. The Arch was moved in 1883 to its present site due to traffic congestion which was still a problem as can be seen in this fabulous 1904 image which is teeming with all manner of horse-drawn vehicles.

In this image some ten years later than the previous photograph, but from a similar and somewhat higher vantage point, the Wellington or Constitution Arch has the Angel of Peace descending on the Quadriga of Victory, which was placed atop the Arch in 1912. Because of this work it was also known as the Victory Arch. It is unusual for a London monument to be known by so many differing names.

This amazing view of Hyde Park from a 1905 postcard has an abundance of open-topped horse omnibuses packed with passengers, travelling on what seems like a very sunny day. Hansom cabs can also be seen either with or plying for customers as they travel around the central square, where today the Wellington Arch stands.

The original Regent Circus, which was renamed Oxford Circus, seen here in this lovely coloured postcard, busy with Londoners going about their business. Not just name changed, but all of the buildings also changed with the rebuilding of Piccadilly Circus and Regent Street between 1895 and 1927. Sadly all of the Nash buildings seen in the image were demolished for the much larger commercial properties we see today.

Located in one of London's most exclusive neighbourhoods of Mayfair, and the subject of a 1940 song and film of the same name, Berkeley Square is today is mostly home to private companies which occupy the grand 18th century terraced town houses once home to London's wealthy gentry. This postcard is from a photographic series of cards of London's wealthy West End residential areas.

A beautifully coloured postcard of Sloane Square in Chelsea which has a four-wheeler and two Hansom cabs waiting for customers at the side of the road. Ths is one London's smarter squares and lies at the east end of the Kings Road. Now an important shopping area, the square was entirely residential when it was laid out in 1771 by Hans Sloane and over the years changed to the busy London square we see today.

LONDON THOROUGHFARES

Fleet Street is a major thoroughfare in central London and was named after the River Fleet which is now covered over and runs underground. Seen here is a view looking towards Ludgate Hill and St. Paul's Cathedral.

Fleet Street has a significant number of monuments and statues along its length, including memorials to important figures from the British press, to which it was once the home. The street is also where the fictitious murderous barber Sweeney Todd lived.

Newgate was one of the historic seven gates of the London Wall defences built around the city, and one of the six which date back to Roman times. Once the gateway itself was used as part of the notorious Newgate Prison. This very nice hand-painted postcard shows the street as the busy thoroughfare it was.

Seen here in this very urban scene of the General Post Office (on the right) is St. Martin's Le Grand, a magnificent street full of stately city buildings. The GPO was the imposing main post office for London between 1829 and 1912, and also the headquarters of the General Post Office of the United Kingdom of Great Britain and Ireland.

High Holborn looking west from Holborn Circus towards the West End. To the east, behind the camera, Holborn Viaduct leads into the city's financial district. Early motor cars are beginning to dominate the London streets, replacing the horse traffic. The statue is of Prince Albert and was commissioned in 1874. Holborn Circus was opened in 1867 and lined with imposing Victorian commercial buildings.

Cheapside in this 1904 image is teeming with pedestrians and horse drawn vehicles, including a Landau style carriage on the extreme left complete with its liveried driver. Cheapside is a major London thoroughfare linking St. Martin's Le Grand with Poultry.

The extremely busy view above is of Holborn looking east and a companion image to the previous image looking west. This clear photographic image show sa London thoroughfare in its hectic daily routine with horses, carts and cabs, motor cars and buses operating in both directions.

107   LONDON. — Corner of Tottenham Court Road. — LL.

This amazingly detailed image of horse omnibuses packed with Londoners on a very active and busy Tottenham Court Road, seen at its junction with Oxford Street and Charing Cross Road. Note the horse bus in the foreground full of gentlemen on its top deck whilst the one behind has mainly ladies with their large and distinctive Edwardian hats.

The Victoria Embankment scheme, along with similar schemes at the Albert Embankment and Chelsea Embankment, were some of London's greatest Victorian improvement programmes. Providing traffic relief for overcrowded streets nearby, the wide tree-lined boulevard opened up space for walking along the Thames. The monumental Somerset House is the large building on the left.

The Strand looking towards the church of St. Mary-Le-Strand is one of the capital's major thoroughfares and runs for just over three quarters of a mile from Trafalgar Square eastwards to Temple Bar, where the road becomes Fleet Street. The Strand is home to Somerset House and many large London hotels such as the Strand Palace and the world renowned Savoy.

The Kingsway Tramway Subway seen above is a cut-and-cover Grade II Listed tunnel in central London, built by the London County Council, and the only one of its kind in Britain. Built in 1898 after clearing slum districts in the Holborn area of the city, it was closed in 1952 when London's trams came to a halt.

Knightsbridge is a very upmarket residential and retail district in West London just south of Hyde Park.

This fantastic photograph shows the Hyde Park Hotel of 1902 on the left, looking east towards Belgravia. Now fully restored it is the Mandarin Oriental Hyde Park and is a high end five-star hotel

Oceanic House still standing today, and now Grade II listed. It was formerly an office building located at 1 Cockspur Street and was completed in 1907. Seen here soon after its completion, this lovely animated postcard view is looking towards the National Gallery. Although a short London thoroughfare, Cockspur Street is very strategically located in central London.

Piccadilly, seen here with Green Park on the left, has been a main road since at least medieval times, and was once known as "the road to Reading". A Robert Baker prospered by making and selling Piccadills (a high stiff collar worn in the 17th century) by fashionable men. His home, Pikadilly Hall, eventually give its name to the street we know today.

Piccadilly became a fashionable place to live and many London mansions were built, particularly in the 18th century. The postcard view above show some of these grand houses, now sadly all gone and replaced by large hotels and commercial buildings.

Whitehall is the main thoroughfare linking Trafalgar Square with Parliament Square. The street is recognised as the centre of the government and is lined with numerous departments and ministries. Consequently, the name "Whitehall" is used as a geographic name for the surrounding area, denoting government.

Looking towards Trafalgar Square, close to the old War Office (on the left). The statue is of Prince George, Duke of Cambridge, one time Commander-in-Chief of the British Army.

Looking in the other direction towards the Houses of Parliament with the Elizabeth tower (Big Ben) and Victoria tower with its flag clearly visible.

WHITEHALL AND THE CENOTAPH. LONDON

This image is also looking in the direction of Trafalgar Square near the the foreign office, taken some years after World War I.

Buildings opposite Marlborough Gate near Hyde Park in fashionable West London, from a card posted in 1905.

This astounding image of The Mall shows almost it's entire length looking towards Buckingham Palace in the far distance. The Mall has long been used for major national ceremonies such as state visits, coronations and funerals, and is a great gathering place especially at the Buckingham Palace end. The surface of The Mall is coloured red to give the effect of a giant red carpet leading up to Palace.

This beautifully coloured Tuck series postcard shows the lovely mansions and London town houses of the rich and famous that once lined Park Lane. Running from Marble Arch to Hyde Park Corner, Park Lane has always been an enclave of the gentry, marking the western boundary of Mayfair. Today it is lined with expensive flats and hotels such as the Dorchester, the Grosvenor House, and the InterContinental.

Looking down on Marble Arch showing the part of Hyde Park that was incorporated to make way for today's dual carriageway. This work also re-appropriated East Carriage Drive inside Hyde Park as the northbound carriageway, moving the park's boundary westwards.

This photograph shows the Royal Palace Hotel in Kensington (now the Royal Garden Hotel) which was demolished and completely rebuilt as the modern hotel building we see today. The gentry of the area can be seen by the two fancy, liveried carriages in the centre of the of the image.

A rare view of Eastbourne Terrace in London's Paddington district, with Paddington Station on the right and the smart houses (now flats and small hotels) on the left. In this lovely postcard view the motorised taxi cabs have taken over from the Hackney and Hansom cabs of previous years.

This pretty 1905 coloured postcard shows Bayswater, which is a major London thoroughfare leading to the western suburbs.

Starting in the east, Bayswater Road originates from the Marble Arch junction and ends in the west at Notting Hill Gate. In this view Bayswater is lined by typical London mansion blocks and town houses facing Hyde Park on the left.

The Victoria Embankment, along with similar schemes at the Albert Embankment and Chelsea Embankment, were some of London's greatest Victorian improvement schemes. Aimed at improving sewage control, as well as providing traffic relief for overcrowded streets nearby, the wide boulevards opened up space for walking along the Thames, with gardens laid out and street lighting for the first time in Britain. Cleopatra's Needle, seen in the background was erected on the Victoria Embankment in 1877.

SHOPPING STREETS

This lovely coloured postcard shows Harrods and its dominant Brompton Road frontage. Located in the very upmarket Knightsbridge, Harrods is a grand building known the world over. Harrods as a business was built up by father and son Charles Henry and Charles Digby Harrod.

In December 1883, following a fire, a new building was built on the site. Rebuilding began again in 1894, and by 1905 the present building we see today took its place as the premier departmental store in London.

London's shops are of course not all grand edifices but comprise many small, localised shops both large and small located all over this vast city. Shopping parades like the one seen here in Baron's Court Terrace in West Kensington were typical of the city then as they are now.

Oxford Circus was as busy a city junction in Edwardian times as it is today with an abundance of horse drawn buses, carriages, carts and cabs travelling in all directions. The massive rebuilding of the old Regency buildings have yet to take place and the old stucco fronted shops and offices still prevail.

Regent Street with its unique curved aspect is a major London shopping street in the heart of the West End. Built in 1825 under the direction of the famous architect John Nash, the street was named after then Prince George, the Prince Regent. Later, in 1830, he become King George IV. Pictured before the redesign of Regent Street was completed in the 1920s, this scene shows the curved part of this famous shopping street. The facades of every building along the street were unified during the redevelopment which started in 1895.

Further up from the curved section of Regent Street this much earlier coloured postcard from 1903 shows an equally busy road, but not a car or motor bus in sight; something which would soon change in the years ahead.

Here in this very clear photograph the old buildings have given way to the much bigger and grander Edwardian buildings that replaced the old stucco fronted and smaller Regency examples. Unlike the previous image, in this picture we see that the motor busses and cars have won the day and are evident here dominating the street, with no horse drawn vehicles anywhere in sight.

This lovely scene in Regent Street, with very elegant ladies out shopping and carriages galore, gives away the clear impression of a busy city. On closer inspection the old, much smaller shops in white stucco can be seen either side of the newer and much grander buildings that were being constructed all along the street during this period.

The long straight stretch of Regent Street seen here has a motor car and carriages competing for road space with one Hansom Cab doing what seems like the Edwardian equivalent of a three-point-turn in the middle of the road. Curious boys seem to have spotted the photographer and are looking directly towards the camera, no doubt happy to be in this lovely image of what to us is now a bygone age.

Oxford Street seen here looking west again shows just how busy a shopping street it has been for most of its existence. This photograph shows just how this street, more than most others in the West End of London, has changed beyond all recognition.

Almost all of the lovely Regency and Victorian buildings seen here have been replaced by huge department stores and large shops in very in modern structures today.

This incredible picture of a New Oxford Street crammed full of horse drawn vehicles of every type is an amazing image of traffic jams which were commonplace even then.

However, there is not a red bus or black cab in sight, but plenty of Edwardian equivalents giving a view of a global metropolis. London at that time was the world's largest city - a title it continued to hold well into the middle of the 20th Century.

LONDON STATIONS

This very colourful Midland Railway postcard of St. Pancras Station states that it has the largest single span railway roof in the world, when in fact it was the largest single span roof structure of any building in the world at the time of its completion in 1868.

The image shows very elegant ladies on the left waiting by the train for its imminent departure to the north.

Euston Station began life as Euston Grove in 1837, growing to serve the line linking London to Birmingham. The building was greatly expanded in 1849 and existed in this form until the modern station building opened in the 1960s. This lovely coloured postcard shows smartly-dressed travellers with members of their families on platforms 13 and 14, ready to board trains to their destinations

The station buildings of London Victoria are seen here before the two mainline station buildings were built during the middle of the Edwardian era. The crowded scene is one from the early 1900s with numerous Hansom cabs waiting at the entrance for customers to emerge. An open top horse omnibus is also visible at bottom right with the driver also ready for his next passengers.

Signs on the station advertise some of the destinations in Europe which can be reached via train and boat from this station.

Victoria station is the mainline station of two northern termini of the Brighton line, the other being London Bridge station.

It is also the terminus of the Chatham main line to Ramsgate and Dover via Chatham. The view here shows the two station buildings side by side, wh the station hotel at extreme the end of the forecourt.

Victoria Station seen here around 1912 now has more motorised vehicles than horse drawn in this very busy scene. Then as now Victoria was a major transport hub connecting the Continent as well as the southern suburbs and beyond to the centre of the city.

The Great Western Hotel on Praed Street in Paddington seen here with a horse drawn bus and two very dapper policemen. This is still is a major London thoroughfare fronting Paddington Station. It was originally laid out in 1828 with town houses for the upper classes, but soon gave way to Victorian enterprise to become a busy shopping street.

The importance of Euston Station grew significantly in the mid- and late-1800s as passenger demand increased. Two hotels could be found adjacent to the station, which later amalgamated into the single Euston Hotel, which flanked Euston Grove, as seen here. The elegant Victorian building offered travellers a place to stay close to the station, but was demolished as Euston was rebuilt and expanded in the 1960s. A busy bus station now occupies the site.

Passengers and station staff stand alongside the 'Down American Special' train at the London and North Western Railway Company's Euston Station in 1910. Built and opened in 1837, it makes Euston the first and thus oldest main railway terminus in London.

Sadly after a long but futile campaign to save it the station, along with the Euston Arch, was demolished in the 1960s and replaced by the very large bland box that we see today.

These two pictures show the importance of London's large station hubs in bringing access to and from the regions. Just as today, hundreds of commuters line every platform awaiting trains, in this case at Paddington Station. Note the various offices and signs along the station wall.

A matt postcard of the train station at Euston which was operated by the London and North Western Railway Company, showing two steam locomotives ready to head north. Platform numbers 1 and 2 seem to be bereft of passengers who may well all be aboard and the trains are ready to depart as the steam emanating from the locomotive on the right may suggest.

Liverpool Street Station was built in 1875 to serve the Great Eastern Railway and its services to destinations such as Norwich, and the East London Railway underground line.

The exterior of the building was of a Gothic design and incorporated the Great Eastern Hotel, seen here, which was opened in 1884. The building was once the only hotel located within the City of London.

The Underground station seen on the left of the picture here in Shepherds Bush is very typical of the architecture of all London Underground station buildings. Usually single storied and quite often tiled on their exterior, these stations were generic in their style and layout and were erected all over the central city. This particular station was built for the new Central Line which was opened in 1900, just a year before Queen Victoria's death.

The Cannon Street's hotel was a five-storey Italianate style city terminus hotel which fronted the station. It was opened in May 1867. The station facade seen here in this coloured postcard from 1909 was very prominent fronting on to Cannon Street and became a city landmark during. Suffering extensive bomb damage after being hit by several incendiary devices during World War II which damaged the roof, the hotel was demolished in 1960.

This incredible overview of both the City of London and the Cannon Street railway station shows the sheer scale of this vast roof which dominates the scene. Built in the mid-1860s the station was a major structure in this part of the city with its 135 ft high twin towers. As can be seen from the image above, the tightly packed roofs and chimneys all seem quite small in comparison.

Cannon Street Station was opened in 1866 and became a major London railway terminus. It is approached across the River Thames by the Cannon Street Railway Bridge, which was built between 1863 and 1866.

These distinctive twin towers flanking the entrance are still standing today, however the main arched structure over the platforms has since been replaced. In this view, from the riverside, the bridge and station are blackened by the years of smoke from both the railways and the city chimneys.

Charing Cross Station on the north bank of the Thames is access from The Strand, and is a unique London terminus in that it is approached by train solely by bridge from across the river. The elegant Charing Cross Hotel greeted passengers. Today the main station building and roof have been replaced by a modern equivalent inspired by this 1864 original structure.

This location is commonly known as the centre of London – the place where all distances to and from the capital are measured.

The spacious booking hall in Waterloo Station where passengers consult timetables and buy tickets for travel to the south west of the country. This particular station has grown into the busiest in the country today, and was for a while the London terminus of the Eurostar service which travels through the Channel Tunnel. This has since moved to St. Pancras Station.

CITY TRANSPORT

The two coloured postcards from King Edward VII's reign showing Charing Cross and Marble Arch, each demonstrating quite clearly the mode of transport for the average working Londoner as being the horse-drawn bus and taxi of the four-wheeler and Hansom cab variety.

The Hansom cab was very popular with Victorian and Edwardian Londoners as a quick and cheap way to get around the city. The driver controlled the horse and drove from the back of the cab. It was an unusual arrangement looking back, but very commonplace at the time. The Hansom cab was made even more famous as the preferred way of getting around by the fictional Sherlock Holmes and Dr. Watson.

This is another amazing image which shows the Bank of England, located on one of the busiest junctions in the London. The scene is jam packed with all manner of horse drawn vehicular traffic, especially open topped omnibuses. On closer inspection, the overwhelming majority of the passengers are male which is no surprise for the time, considering it is in the heart of the commercial city.

A similar scene to the previous image but with a wider viewpoint of the Bank of England showing its showgrounds with the Royal Exchange to the right and Threadneedle Street in-between. Once again the traffic is heavy as they travel past the "Old Lady of Threadneedle Street" as the Bank was and still is affectionately known.

A lovely coloured image of Ludgate Circus, here seen in the Edwardian heyday. It was a very busy London Junction at the bottom of Fleet Street. The railway bridge once led to Ludgate Hill station but has now been removed, creating a uninterrupted view up Ludgate Hill towards the main entrance to St. Paul's Cathedral.

LONDON.
THE NATIONAL GALLERY.
(A Wet Day in Town).

This pretty painted postcard of a Hansom cab seen here in Duncannon Street, just off Trafalgar Square, depicts a rainy yet atmospheric street scene.

Hansom cabs enjoyed immense popularity as they were fast, light enough to be pulled by a single horse (making the journey cheaper than travelling in a larger four-wheel coach) and were agile enough to steer around horse-drawn vehicles in the notorious traffic jams of nineteenth-century London. There were up to 7,500 hansom cabs in use at the height of their popularity.

Fleet Street was once home to the country's national newspapers, but is now just another busy central London thoroughfare. Here, as with so many of the capital's roads, it is busy with omnibuses traveling in both directions, and passengers - both ladies and gentlemen - enjoying their journey on what seems like a lovely dry day.

This beautifully photographed and informative postcard gives a study of the horse-drawn omnibus, which was so prevalent as a means of public transport in London until the motor-bus, tram and Underground came into use superseding this somewhat quaint mode of city travel. It is quite amazing to think that they were never covered during the vast majority of their existence and thus totally open to all the elements of the inclement British weather.

This wonderful picture of a London & North Western Railway horse-drawn omnibus also commonly found on the capitols street. Note the luggage and bicycles being carried on the roof of the vehicle, and the blanket to keep the driver and riders warm and hopefully a little dry in case of rain.

A wonderful photograph of Regent Street with three Hansom cabs plying for passengers in close proximity. The Hansom cab was a unique horse-drawn carriage as the driver was seated at the rear end of the cab which seems to the modern viewer quite a difficult thing to do. It was designed and patented in 1834 by Joseph Hansom, hence its name. Note the lovely shop fronts along Regent Street which were soon to be demolished for the grander edifices which today line the whole street.

Although night photography was not possible in Edwardian England, it didn't stop the postcard manufactures from depicting evening and night time scenes as seen here in this early postcard from around 1907. This night view of The National Gallery in Trafalgar Square has Hackney and Hansom cabs plus two London horse buses all busily on their way on a moonlit night.

The Eleanor Cross,
From Charing-Cross Station-yard
London.

This is not the actual site of the accepted centre of London, known as Charing Cross as that was close by and nearer to Trafalgar Square. However, following the construction of the replica Eleanor Cross and Charing Cross railway station in 1864, the station forecourt where the cross was re-sited became more commonly associated with the centre of the city.

The following three images show very nice examples of the charabanc or (often pronounced "sharra-bang") which were a type of horse-drawn vehicle and early motor coach. They were almost always open-topped, carrying their passengers in the open air. This particular example is seen waiting outside Copp's Coach & Bus Office and is ready to depart, full to the brim with it's well dressed passengers who are posing proudly for the photographer.

This charabanc is carrying both ladies and gentlemen, with children and even a dog also ready to depart for a day out to either the seaside or maybe out the countryside. The eager passengers are all facing the same way (quite often they faced each other) and although usually only used for day trips charabancs were often seen around the city on their journeys to the hinterland around London.

This beautifully crafted charabanc is a much larger example to the two previous images and here it has bench seats arranged in rows, commonly used for large parties, whether for public conveyances or for excursions in and around the city, seaside or countryside. This wonderful image shows just how popular they were and is packed with some 18 passengers and a driver. The charabanc is advertising The Times newspaper.

Although rare in the city, this fantastically regal coach and horses seems to have a crest on the door which may well be of the nobility who all had town houses in London. As such they were regularly seen around the city, especially in the western areas such as Kensington, Chelsea, Mayfair or Belgravia. A liveried driver and two footmen wearing top hats give this particular coach a further aristocratic look on their drives around the city or in Hyde Park - a favourite venue to show off one's wealth.

London Bridge looking quite new in this stunning scene from 1902. This is because by 1896 the bridge was the busiest point in London and one of its most congested, with up to 8,000 pedestrians and 900 vehicles crossing every hour at peak periods. As such the bridge was widened by some 13 feet using granite corbels before the turn of the century. This work has given the bridge a new look in this image. Even though horse drawn, the impact of this vehicular traffic is evident in the amazing photograph above.

The first electric line over Westminster Bridge opened in May 1903, the route travelling between the bridge and Tooting.

In this photograph of the bridge from 1905 the view is looking south towards St. Thomas' Hospital in Lambeth, with the newer double decker trams on the left and the older horse omnibus seen on right. Together with early cars and a Hansom cab, behind which is a motorised bus, it is an interesting mix of the older and newer types of London's road transport together and capturing them all in one unique image.

In this busy scene teeming with vehicular traffic travelling over Blackfriars Bridge around 1905, two double decker electric trams can be seen on the bridge, with one just coming into view in the far distance. Three London omnibuses can also be seen.

The first fully operational electric tram electric tramway system was introduced in 1901 by Croydon Corporation and by 1903 there over were 300 electric tramcars in London, which carried 800,000 passengers over one Whitsun weekend as early as 1903.

Another marvellous scene from a similar vantage point as the previous image, but now showing 1913 where motorised omnibuses dominate the scene. The demise of the horse buses had been gradual, but by the time of the outbreak of Great War of 1914-18 they had ceased to be in operation. The last recorded horse omnibus in London was a Tilling bus which last ran between Peckham and Honor Oak Tavern, on 4 August 1914.

Motorised public transport in London ran for many years side by side with the old horse drawn variety, with electric trams and motor buses eventually replacing the them. Although horse drawn cabs continued until the early 1920s, motorised taxicabs started plying London streets as early as 1897 when 25 were introduced, and by 1898 there were 50 more. Early motor cars were making their appearance by the mid-1890s and by the beginning of World War I were an increasing dominant presence.

However, the motor car was still the preserve of the rich and famous, and although most were only in the big cities, London had the vast majority and were to be seen especially in the central and western part of the city. This lovely postcard, one of a series, shows a typical chauffeur at the wheel of a car outside what seems like a hotel.

Actors and actresses were avid car owners and were often seen around town in their chauffeur driven vehicles.

Here, in this very posed image, is the American-born actress Miss Billy Burke, who was on stage in London around the time of this postcard from 1904.

A remarkable view depicting upper class wealth, with chauffeur and footman stood by their employer's new motor car and servants looking on from front entrance of this grand London town house.

HAMPSTEAD. — FINCHLEY ROAD & FROGNAL STATION.

A fascinating coloured postcard from 1905, unintentionally showing the old verses the new on the roads of Edwardian England.

The motor car seems to be racing against the old horse drawn omnibus, which is slowly making its way past Finchley Road & Frognal Station in Hampstead, which today is in the Borough of Camden.

LONDON LIFE

Very integral to London life in the Edwardian era was the hotel, as it was a place not just to stay, but to meet and socialise, especially for the rich and famous, as well as the growing middle classes. The London hotel then, as today, was a place that had fabulous restaurants and sumptuous reception rooms in which to meet, along with grand public lobbies where you could be seen in all your finery.

The First Avenue Hotel in Holborn was one of London's premier hotels but was completely destroyed by the Luftwaffe in the Blitz of World War II.

Not far from Buckingham Palace and adjoining Victoria Station, the Grosvenor Hotel was typical of the grand station hotels associated with the larger London railway termini. This beautifully coloured postcard has an almost Parisian look about it. The building stills stands today and has retained its original name, but is now part of the luxury Guoman Hotels chain.

The Ritz Hotel was always a very up-market establishment and a favourite meeting place for the rich and famous of the London gentry, as well as the more discerning visitor. It was and still is a 5 Star and Grade II listed hotel. It can be found in London's prestigious Piccadilly.

The Ritz Club in the basement contains the world renowned casino, a feature of the hotel from its inception, although originally located in the Ritz ballroom upon the opening in May 1906.

The Royal Palace Hotel was situated on the edge of Kensington Gardens. This sophisticated establishment is now known as the Royal Garden Hotel and today occupies a 1960s glass-and-stone building, replacing the original seen in this old coloured postcard, which was demolished. Always very popular with upper-class Londoners and tourists alike due to being only a five minute walk from High Street Kensington, with its shops, restaurants and Tube station.

The Gaiety Theatre was a London West End theatre located on Aldwych at the eastern end of The Strand. On the former site of the Lyceum Theatre, it became known as the Gaiety Theatre in 1868 and was, at first, known for music hall and then became famous for musical burlesque, pantomime and operetta performances. It closed in 1939 and was eventually demolished. The theatre building is seen in this old postcard view looking down Aldwych on a very prominent site.

A closer image of the entrance to the Gaiety Theatre showing the busy street and well known actresses of the day Gabriella Ray, Gertie Millar and Marie Studholme smiling to the viewer from across the front of the postcard.

One of the largest and grandest of the West End theatres was the London Hippodrome, still standing today and now operating as a large casino.

Opening at the turn of the century in 1900, the building has been used for many different entertainments such as theatres, music halls, bingo prior to its present occupation.

This early postcard shows the Hippodrome in all its architectural grandeur on its corner location at Cranbourn Street and Charing Cross Road. The name Hippodrome was derived from animal acts which once formed a significant part of the entertainment, and was used for theatres across the country.

The London Life series were a wonderful collection of postcards showing the various lifestyles of Londoners in scenes around the city. In this card we see enthusiastic opera followers in a queue outside the Royal Opera House in Covent Garden. The early birds have obviously organised themselves ready for a long wait as evident by the fact they are sitting on folding seats.

This Wonderful scene of the main Covent Garden Market building, which on first glance isn't too different to today, is complete with Edwardian barrow boys and the general population shopping at the stalls. The Market buildings were saved from demolition in the 1970s to be restored and enhanced for us to enjoy today. With its restaurants, shops and street entertainers Covent Garden is now a very lively, vibrant and a much loved part of central London.

London Zoo is the world's oldest scientific zoo. It was opened in London on 27 April 1828, and was originally intended to be used as a collection for scientific study. Then, as now, it was a very popular day out for Londoners as well as visitors to the city.

This lovely coloured postcard depicts a familiar scene for an elephant ride and shows ladies and girls in their long flowing dresses, some already seated whilst others are waiting for their turn.

Sunday Morning in Wentworth Street.

The Law Courts.

A Sunday Morning in Wentworth Street with its teeming market, better known as Petticoat Lane Market, followed by a historic image of the 1870s Law Courts on The Strand.

This series of Edwardian postcards always had a London Policeman, Fireman or Postman on the card with their image usually on the side of the main picture.

London Zoo is the world's oldest scientific zoo. It was opened in London on 27 April 1828, and was originally intended to be used as a collection for scientific study. Then, as now, it was a very popular day out for Londoners as well as visitors to the city.

This lovely coloured postcard depicts a familiar scene for an elephant ride and shows ladies and girls in their long flowing dresses, some already seated whilst others are waiting for their turn.

Founded in London by wax sculptor Marie Tussaud as early as 1835, Madame Tussauds has become one of London's premier tourist attractions, displaying lifelike waxwork models of celebrities and famous people. As can been seen in the image above, it has always attracted crowds and to this day has very long queues outside its main building on Marylebone Road. Madame Tussaud's grandson, Joseph Randall, commissioned the building.

A favourite London pastime was feeding the pigeons in Trafalgar Square and outside St. Paul's Cathedral. Millions of people over the years have enjoyed this simple pleasure and had their photograph taken with the pigeons on their arms. It was even popularised in the Disney film Mary Poppins, making it a ritual known worldwide.

Sadly, the act is now banned by a recently introduced bylawby the City of Westminster, under which anyone feeding birds risks a £500 fine.

Shoe polish was not well known as a commercial product until the early 20th Century. As such, shoeshine boys and men were commonplace by the late 19th Century and plied their trade on the streets of cities across the United Kingdom, with London in particular having a large number. The chap here having his shoe polished is a London cab driver, evident by the license on his coat lapel.

Grosvenor Square in Mayfair was laid out in the early 1700s and quickly became one of the most fashionable addresses to live in London. Its sides are lined by these grand houses, each designed individually, and at one time home to the aristocracy. The United States Embassy occupied a site in Grosvenor Square until 2009.

The term 'flower girl' was commonly used to refer to young females who would scatter flower petals down the aisle during a wedding procession. However, the term is more commonly used to refer to girls who sold flowers, especially in Victorian and Edwardian times. The most famous such flower girl was the fictional character Eliza Doolittle from the play Pygmalion. In the coloured postcard above two ladies are selling their roses on a busy London street, with one young lady customer searching her purse ready to pay the seller.

In this wonderfully atmospheric postcard we see a somewhat mature flower lady selling her flowers by Hyde Park Corner. A pipe smoking gentleman seems quite immersed in choosing whilst the seller seems looks on indifferently. During the Victorian and Edwardian period these flower sellers had their prime pitches staked out at well-known and busy locations to capture passing trade.

A "Street Orderly Boy" is an old name for a street cleaner. These were sweepers and cleaners of horse manure and were a common sight in London during the 19th and early 20th centuries. This particular fellow on the London Types series of postcards seems very young to be working, but was a common sight at the time.

A London Postman.

The Wrench Series. No. 1031.

Another series of Londoners and their jobs was produced by the Wrench series of postcards, including this plain but effective 1907 card showing a very smart London Postman, posing quite nonchalantly in his fine Royal Mail uniform. The series featured, firemen, policemen and many other London professions.

Piccadilly showing the Duke of Devonshire's House. LONDON. *le 24. November 1903*

Lieber Lolli: Nach einem phaktischen mal de mer glücklich in London angekommen. Wir sind wahrlich Donnerstag oder Freitag schon wieder in Paris. Herzl. Grüße Anna Kirsch

1983.

The Grand London Mansions of the British gentry, built mainly in the 18th and 19th centuries, were plentiful in London and set in prime locations. The postcard here shows the Duke of Devonshire's London home on Piccadilly – a mansion which was completed 1740, but stood empty after World War I and was demolished in 1924. Today the site is occupied by an office building known as Devonshire House.

174   LONDON W. — Park Lane, Stanhope Gate. — LL.

This busy view of Stanhope Gate (incorrectly spelled on the postcard) on London's prestigious Park Lane shows Dorchester House, one such beautiful mansion which has since been demolished to make way for The Dorchester Hotel, built in 1931. The hotel has become one of the world's most prestigious and expensive hotels.

The London town house is unique to the capital, acting as the homes of the rich and upper classes from the 18th to the early 20th centuries. With their usually white stucco façades, these tall terraced structures averaged five-to-seven floors, including a basement level. The examples that follow are typical London town houses which would be found in the wealthier parts of the city but particularly in the West and South West, where they still dominate the urban landscape.

J. S. 41. **Hertford House (Wallace Collection). Manchester Square, London.**

Hertford House was a grand London mansion. It was the former home of the Seymour family and today houses The Wallace Collection, which is a vast collection of art, furniture, armour and other historic objects. The postcard view above shows the mansion, one of only a few such London mansions of the gentry to survive, in its quiet and sedate location on the north side of Manchester Square.

Boasting five floors and a basement, the elegant terraced houses of Queen's Gardens in Bayswater have always been an exclusive place to live in the city.

Rutland Gate is another upmarket Kensington address where today a small flat can easily cost £2 million. In this original scene, however, the houses would have been occupied by a single family and their servant staff.

The term 'Hackney Carriage', used to describe the taxis found in London, is not, as the name suggests, anything to do with the village (and now suburb) of the same name. The term Hackney is thought to derive from the type of horse used to pull cabs, as seen here in the early 1900s.

This London home has the lady of the house (in all her finery) with two companions or servants standing quite proudly above the main portico entrance. They are clearly posing for the photographer who seems to be positioned in a property opposite.

This rather grand and elegant six-storied town house has very tall and prominent chimneys, somewhat unusual for London properties such as these. It also has a mini balustrade around the main entrance level and stone walls rather than railings at the front of the house leading down to the basement. A fancy modern motor car stands ready and waiting for the house inhabitants to come out and be chauffeured around town.

A servant girl stands outside her employer's home, only slightly taller than the railings. These railings were an integral part of every London town house but many were ripped up during World War II to supply the supposed demand for metal. However, this was rarely the case and simply a morale boosting war campaign which cost these houses their historic railings, some of which were over a hundred years old.

This smaller than the average town house is only four floors, including its basement. It has the usual white stucco façade, but also a brick effect on the main entrance level, giving it a distinguished look.

RIVER SCENES

A lovely collectable coloured postcard showing a very dominant St. Pauls Cathedral looming over the riverscape with a steam ferryboat on the river and a long plume of smoke bellowing from its funnel. These type of stylised picturesque postcards was very popular in the Edwardian era and they were produced and posted in their millions.

A pretty coloured postcard from 1907 showing the river at the Victoria Embankment and Waterloo Bridge.

Victoria Embankment was built between 1865 and 1870 and before it was built the river came right up to the Neoclassical Somerset house, also shown here.

A grand view of the River Thames seen from the south bank close to Lambeth Palace. The Palace of Westminster can be seen in it's wonderful location on the north bank of the river with its commanding presence. This building was a replacement for the much older Palace of Whitehall which contained the Parliament building amongst many others, and the present grand building was built after that original was burnt to the ground in 1834.

Better known as the Houses of Parliament with its famous towers of Victoria and the new renamed Elizabeth Tower which houses the clock tower and its bell – known the world over as Big Ben.

Lambeth Palace seen here from the River Thames is the residence of the Archbishop of Canterbury. Clearly seen here is the main early Tudor Gatehouse which was built by Cardinal John Morton and completed in 1495. It is located on the south bank of the River Thames to the west of Westminster Bridge.

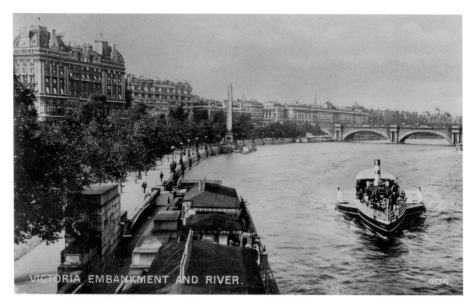

This photographic postcard view of the Victoria Embankment in mid-summer shows the riverbank in all its glory with its avenue of trees along the entire length. A Thames ferry packed with passengers glides towards the river pier on the north bank.

This view of the River Thames looking over towards the City and St. Paul's shows a still very dominant Cathedral looming over the wharves and buildings of this part of London, as it has done for over 300 years. Only the Victorian commercial wharves seen on the riverfront show a city that was changing. Within a generation this London scene would be consigned to History.

This pleasing view of St. Pauls Cathedral is taken from the Southwark side of the Thames and depicts an ever changing and picturesque scene, and a source of interest with the Thames barges and other shipping showing some of the busy river activity.

A 150 Ton floating crane seen here in the process of lifting a railway carriage with ease in this unusual postcard.

Owing to its sheer size this particular crane had the nickname "London Mammoth" which was apt given its giant proportions.

A fantastic overview of the London skyline looking towards Blackfriars Bridge and railway station, and northwards to St. Pauls Cathedral.

This marvellously busy and active river scene is taken from Tower Bridge looking over the City of London towards St. Paul's in the distance, behind the roof of Cannon Street railway station. The Monument to the Great Fire of 1666 can be seen just to the right of the dome of the Cathedral.

 The Thames here is full of river traffic and shows just how busy the river was in the years just before the Great War of 1914-1918.

This view of the River Thames looking over the City and showing a cityscape still very much as it has been for centuries. Tower Bridge looms over the river, with the Tower of London to the left. As the text on the card testifies, this view is taken from the top of the Monument.

In this wonderfully evocative view of Tower Bridge from London Bridge one can see that large vessels still came into the Pool of London during this period. Though the quays and wharves here suffered very heavy bomb damage during World War II they continued to function until the start of redevelopment in the 1960s. The Tower of London is out of view but is located on the middle left in this 1911 postcard.

This view of the City of London from Tower Bridge is similar to the previous view, but taken further upstream and many years earlier. It shows the City dominated by both St. Paul's and the roofline of Cannon Street Station and also the many city churches with towers and spires built by Christopher Wren, and still piercing the London skyline as they had done so since the late 17th Century.

The Tower of London showing its commanding position on the river watching over the approach to the city, standing guard since it was built by William The Conqueror in 1078. This clear photographic postcard shows the Traitor's Gate on the extreme left and from where access to the Tower was once directly possible from the River Thames.

Although actually located off the river, the Thame side enclosed docks were once the greatest dock system in the world and a mention must be made of them. Stretching for miles on both banks of the river these docks made London the largest port in the world. Started in the 1790s they were enlarged from 1802.

They included the West India Docks (1802), East India Docks (1805), Surrey Commercial Docks (1807), St Katharine Docks (1828), Royal Victoria Dock (1855), Millwall Dock (1868), Royal Albert Dock (1880), and Tilbury docks (1886)to name but a few.

This amazing image shows countless ships in the Royal Albert Dock with their cargoes from around the world ready to be off loaded, ready for market.

This truly beautiful image from 1907 shows the Greenwich Royal Naval College as seen from the Thames. Today this is a World Heritage Site owing to the significance of the architecture and its location. The Sir Christopher Wren-designed buildings were originally a hospital built in 1696, which then became a Naval training college.

LONDON BRIDGES

These two very contrasting images of London Bridge show the diversity of London life in all its glory. It also shows the variety of postcard scenes available at the time, from the wonderfully coloured ones to matt finish types and the real photographic examples. Postcards from London were sent in their millions during the heyday period from 1895 to 1920.

Old London Bridge (this one being the third only on the site in just over 2,000 years) is just upstream of its better known neighbour Tower Bridge, with which London Bridge is often confused. After the wooden Roman bridge, there stood the Medieval Bridge (1209-1931) covered with houses, shops and chapels. This was replaced by the bridge seen above. Subsequently this very bridge was then dismantled after 140 years of use and sold to the USA where it was reconstructed piece by piece in Lake Havasu City, Arizona in 1971. The current three span bridge on the same site was opened in March 1973 by Queen Elizabeth II.

Looking across from the City of London southwards to Southwark. London Bridge is thronged with traffic as it can be today. Vehicles are jammed in both directions and just as today pedestrians are densely packed walking across the bridge. Southwark Cathedral can be seen with its 15th Century central tower looming over the misty skyline.

A lovely panoramic view of Westminster Bridge looking northwards with the Palace of Westminster (better known as the Houses of Parliament) dominating the north bank of the Thames since it's completion in the mid 1850s. It replaced the Palace of Whitehall which was burnt down in 1834, with its most famous architectural feature being the newly named Elizabeth Tower, better known as Big Ben. The world-renowned New Scotland Yard headquarters building can also be seen (the last building on the right).

Looking in the opposite direction across Westminster Bridge towards the new County Hall, completed in 1922, with additions later added. Today it is the home of the London Sea Life Aquarium and the London Eye big wheel attraction.

Looking south towards the Borough of Lambeth, this wonderful postcard shows the buildings of St. Thomas' Hospital. Motorised open topped busses and double decker trams are seen travelling in both directions over Westminster Bridge. St. Thomas' is one of London's most famous hospitals and is associated with many famous names, chief among them being Florence Nightingale. It is also as a very prominent London landmark, largely due to its location on the opposite bank of the River Thames to the Houses of Parliament.

Known the world over, Tower Bridge is seen here with the famous roadway in its down position, allowing traffic to cross the River Thames. In the foreground, a typical Thames barge lies upstream with its sail unfurled.

Built in late Victorian times the bridge was opened in 1894 and soon became one of London's most famous architectural icons, loved by Londoners and visitors alike.

Here a contrasting scene showing the bridge's roadway is in the up, or raised, position with a few large vessels travelling downstream towards the outer docks and the North Sea. Smaller rowing boats in contrast to the much larger ships show the sheer size of what could travel under the bridge with roadway raised.

This very detailed early picture of the entrance to Tower bridge shows a rare close up of Edwardian Londoners on their travels around the city. To the modern onlooker it seems unbelievable given the poor British weather that all the early busses (both horse drawn and motorised) were open topped. Many delivery carts and wagons are crossing in this scene, as well as the famous Hansom Cabs which were then equivalent of today's London's Black Cabs. It seems some of the drivers and bus passengers are aware of the photographer as they are inquisitively looking in his direction.

This lovely postcard from around 1907 shows the Tower of London looming over the River Thames with Tower Bridge's roadway in the foreground, making a very interesting view. At the time the bridge was a new addition to London's landmarks having been opened only 11 years prior to this picture. The image has been taken from the southern approach to the bridge with a part of the northern approach Tower just visible on the right through the archway.

The elegant Hammersmith suspension bridge. The single early motorcar here is a stark contrast to the volume of traffic using the bridge today, which has caused numerous structural issues.

ROYAL LONDON

The Tudor St. James's Palace was built in red brick during the reign of Henry VIII, mostly between 1531 and 1536, and acted as a royal residence till queen Victoria moved to Buckingham Palace in 1837.

Today the palace houses a number of official offices, societies and collections and all Ambassadors and High commissioners to the United Kingdom are still accredited to the Court of St James.

This atmospheric photographic postcard of Buckingham Palace showing the original East Wing built in 1847-50, which was demolished to make way for the facade that we see today, which dates from 1913. Here we see carriages and a Hansom Cab driving by, and to their right is the area where the yet to be built Victoria Memorial will occupy.

Yeoman Warders of the Tower, Tower of London

The Yeomen Warders of the Tower of London are seen here in all their finery wearing the uniforms that go back to the Tudor era.

They are the Sovereign's Body Guard and are known as The Yeoman Guard Extraordinary, and have two distinct uniforms. One is the Yeomen Tudor State Uniform shown in the image above, and the other is the everyday dress uniform.

The Yeomen Warders were formed in 1485 by the new King Henry VII, the first monarch of the Tudor dynasty. Popularly known as the Beefeaters, they are to this day the ceremonial guardians of the Tower of London.

L.470. LONDON. HORSE GUARDS PARADE – JUDGES' LT?

This beautiful postcard shows a timeless scene which is the same today as seen in this lovely scene.

Here we see The Blues and Royals (Royal Horse Guards and 1st Dragoons) which is a cavalry regiment of the British Army and is part of the well-known Household Cavalry which are so popular with Londoners as well as tourists from all over the world.

Here in this busy image we can see the Household Cavalry within the courtyard of the Horse Guards building fronting Whitehall.

The Blues and Royals is one of two regiments of the Household Division and ride to and from Buckingham Palace along The Mall on ceremonial duties to the delight of visitors.

The Horse Guards building fronting Whitehall is an 18th Century edifice which has long been a very popular spot for tourists to stand beside the mounted guards and take photographs ever since Victorian times.

The building itself is a large Grade I listed historical structure in the Palladian style, and is situated between Whitehall and Horse Guards Parade.

The main Whitehall frontage of the Horse Guards building showing the inner courtyard where we can see the Household Cavalry lined up to perform their ceremonial duties. Tourists are gathering at the main gate to view the goings on inside.

Buckingham Palace seen here looks quite serene and grand in this early Edwardian image. The rebuilding of the famous East Wing we are familiar with was not commenced until 1912-3 and here the Victorian East Wing of 1847-50 is still present. Note there is no Victoria Memorial monument in place yet, which was not built until 1911.

Note the elegant carriage seen here on the right with its smart driver and horses.

This wonderfully animated real photographic postcard shows the old façade of Buckingham Palace, with the Victorian East Wing, which was demolished a couple of years after this image was taken - most likely soon after the official opening of the Victoria Memorial monument as stated on the postcard text on the 16th of May 1911.

It is a marvellous view of the new monument as well as a good contrast showing of the older carriages with the newer motor cars which would soon displace them in the years ahead.

In this wonderfully clear view we can now see the new East Wing of Buckingham Palace that we know and are familiar with today.

Taken on what seems like an early morning on a wet day the image depicts quite a surreal appearance being devoid of life and looking somewhat foreboding, yet beautiful in its serenity.

Buckingham Palace and Queen Victoria Memorial. 313.

A lighter and more inviting scene of the Palace with the Household Cavalry of the Blues and Royals riding by the Victoria Memorial, on what seems like a crowdless day. However, the crowds are here in great numbers behind the camera.

This very rural view of Kensington Palace with grazing sheep in front shows the late 17th Century part of the Palace which was the home of many monarchs until Queen Victoria moved the official royal residence to Buckingham Palace. Queen Victoria was born in Kensington Palace and was here in 1837 when, known then as Princess Alexandrina Victoria, she was awakened to be told that her uncle, King William IV, had died and that she was now queen.

LONDON PARKS

Situated along the south side of Hyde Park in central London, Rotten Row leads from Hyde Park Corner to the Serpentine Road. During the 18th and 19th centuries, Rotten Row was a very fashionable place for rich and upper-class Londoners, where they could be seen horse riding as in this colourful postcard. Note the Lady riding side saddle.

Today it is still maintained as a place to ride horses in the centre of London, but in these modern times it is sadly little used for this purpose.

In this marvellous photographic postcard view of Rotten Row we see gentlemen wearing top hats plus a very large crowd of seated Londoners enjoying the summer weather, whilst riders and even a distance carriage use the thoroughfare.

The very ornate entrance gates to the vast Hyde Park, here on the north side of the park at Marble Arch. "Posh" carriages and early motor cars enter and leave the park through five pillared entrances onto the broad carriageway. At bottom-right a Hansom cab vies with an early 1900s motor car in a foretaste of the changes ahead when all horse drawn vehicles will give way to motorised transport.

Another great photographic image, and again a sign of the future as a motor car is seen here side-by-side with a very high class and elegant carriage. Rotten Row can be seen in all its beauty in the heart of London. Wide pedestrian carriageways on both sides give ample space for the gentry to walk, amble and observe the richer folk glide by in their carriages.

On the south side of Hyde Park and within the gates seen here at Hyde Park Corner, the richer populous of London are out and about on this very hot summers day, evidenced by the many umbrellas being used for shade by the ladies on the left. Here as on the north side at the Marble Arch entrance carriages travel in and out at speed with their rich occupants enjoying a drive to show off their wealth.

This 1905 image of Hyde Park showing just how busy it was on a lovely, sunny summer day where countless carriages vie for space in this traffic jam of horses and carriages, all attended by liveried drivers and footmen. Here the wealth on display is immense as these carriages are the Rolls Royce's and Mercedes of their day, and many of the carriages have not one but two servants per carriage.

The more middle-class Londoners from the city are on show as here along the Broad Walk in Hyde Park, ambling in their finery with nannies and ladies in their large Edwardian hats clearly seen here in this 1912 real photo postcard.

The Serpentine (officially known as the Serpentine River) is a 40-acre recreational lake in Hyde Park and was created in 1730 at the behest of Queen Caroline. The lake is a very popular body of water for boating and bathing within the park. Londoners of all classes made it a very integral part of their day out on visits to Hyde Park, especially on the hot summer days.

In this very sedate picture postcard view of the Serpentine we can see the Serpentine Bridge which marks the boundary between Hyde Park and Kensington Gardens and also marks the Serpentine's western boundary. The long and narrow western half of the lake is known as the Long Water. The Serpentine itself takes its name from its snakelike and curving shape, even though it only has one bend.

A lovely view looking from inside Hyde Park towards Marble Arch in the middle distance. Two carriages, with one having two servants and the other with just, one are being driven around the park with their occupants enjoying a fine day.

Top hats and uniformed drivers show the off their employers' wealth and elegance, most likely from the London gentry.

Green Park, although one of the smaller of the Royal Parks of London, is nevertheless a beautiful green lung in the heart of the city.

Officially located in the City of Westminster, Green Park has fine mansions fronting it including Clarence House and Spencer House, but it does not have any lakes, buildings or playgrounds and only a few monuments. This view shows the newly completed Victoria Memorial which opened in 1911.

The one thing Green Park did have was a very popular bandstand, seen here in this photographic postcard from 1912. Men in their summer boater hats are gathered, most likely to listen to a summer concert.

Between 1865 and 1870 when the northern Embankment and sewer were built by Sir Joseph Bazalgette, there were no gardens here. They followed in 1874 when created on the reclaimed land on the inward side of the roadway in honour of the queen, and named Victoria Embankment. Then as now the gardens were a very popular place to stroll and rest from the teeming city behind the buildings on The Strand, many of which have long been replaced from this view.

Regents Park is one of the larger of the Royal Parks of London and named after the Prince Regent, later King George IV, who commissioned it in 1811. There are grand terraces flanking the park and it has a grandeur all of its own. Located with the park's boundary is London zoo, which was opened in 1828 and is the world's oldest scientific zoo. Today it is still one of the largest in the world with over 17,450 animals, some which can only be seen there.

The elephant rides were very popular in Victorian and Edwardian times. In 1865, Jumbo, the largest elephant known at the time, came to the zoo. His name became an epithet for anything of a large size, such as the Boeing's 747 Jumbo Jet.

SPECIAL EVENTS

During the period 1900 to 1918 there were many special occasions, ranging from Queen Victoria and King Edward's state funerals to the coronations of King Edward VIII and King George V. There were also many important exhibitions and fairs and royal visits to the city.

These two beautifully coloured images depict the 1908 Franco - British Exhibition, which was in the same year that the fourth Olympics of the modern era were also held in London.

NELSON DAY.

The great crowd in Trafalgar Square, October 21st, 1905, paying its tribute to the national hero. It is calculated that nearly 1,000,000 persons, of every age, sex and condition, visited the great sailor's monument.

The 1805 Battle of Trafalgar was commemorated by the building of Nelson's Column. Here on the 100th anniversary of the battle we see fantastic crowds gathered in Trafalgar Square to honour Admiral Nelson and remember the great battle. The text on the postcard speaks for itself.

A pageant of crowded yachts, steamers and boats of all sizes are gathered here at Tower Bridge in this busy River Thames view.

73. THAMES NAVAL PAGEANT. JULY '09.
TORPEDO BOATS NEAR WESTMINSTER. - JUDGES

A view of the Palace of Westminster during the summer of 1909 when the Royal Navy fleet was gathered on the River Thames in a great pageant. It was the week of Saturday 17-24 and ships from the Home and Atlantic Fleets were moored along the Thames from Westminster Bridge to the Nore Lightship in the estuary, some 45 miles in total.

L.70. THAMES NAVAL PAGEANT. JULY '09.
SCENE FROM WESTMINSTER - JUDGES'

LONDON COUNTY COUNCIL

The Thames Naval Pageant of July 1909 was a major event, as was reported elsewhere "Never before in the history of nations has there been so remarkable an assembly of warships as that gathered here together on the Thames" in this glorious summer.

Great processions during the years from 1900 to 1919 were quite common with the deaths of Queen Victoria and King Edward VII, as well as the coronations of kings Edward VII and George V. Loyal troops from across the Empire were sent to join these very lavish occasions which were huge events, as can be seen by this wonderful image showing the funeral of Queen Victoria.

WOOD LANE ENTRANCE   JAPAN-BRITISH EXHIBITION

The Japan-British Exhibition took place at the specially constructed, so-called White City in London from 14 May to 29 October 1910. It included all manner of exhibition halls and purpose-built buildings. This real photograph shows the very ornate Wood Lane entrance.

It was the largest international exposition that the Empire of Japan ever attended up to that date and was a great success, drawing massive crowds throughout.

This beautiful and very grand entrance was the main entry into the Franco-British Exhibition of 1908. The lovely tall towers and gleaming white stucco gave the exhibition buildings a very pleasing aspect in the otherwise dull British weather. This gateway fronted Shepherds Bush Green and survived well into the present, being demolished in 1999 for the Westfield shopping centre development.

The Empire Exhibition held at Wembley Park between April 1924 and October 1925 as a means of strengthening the bond between Britain and the rest of the Empire, which had been slipping since the end of World War I. One major aspect of the Exhibition was the building of a new 'Empire Stadium'. This would later become Wembley Stadium, with its iconic towers seen here. It would go on to host many important sporting events, including the 1948 Summer Olympics and 1966 World Cup. The stadium was replaced in the early 2000s.

The Court of Honour at the Franco-British Exhibition was a very impressive architectural statement and a great area in which to gather and enjoy the sights and amble around the buildings and lake. The oriental style of the exhibition buildings and their whiteness combined to make a very impressive and exotic ensemble.

Of the many beautiful buildings constructed for the Franco-British Exhibition was the fabulous Applied Arts Palace, which with its two immense towers and very grand domed entrance was a landmark structure of some considerable grandeur. With lovely gardens fronting this entrance the setting made a lasting impression upon any visitor.

The Flip-Flap, from Elite Gardens,
Franco-British Exhibition, London, 1908.

The attraction that captivated Londoners the most to the 1908 exhibition was the giant Flip-Flap ride, which at the time was a great novelty and a fantastic thrill for all those who dared to venture upon it. This rather lovely picture taken from the Elite Gardens shows the elegance of the Edwardian Ladies with their long dresses and large hats.

A very rare and unusual birds eye view of the Franco-British Exhibition with the photograph having been taken from a balloon high above the stadium. The sprawling exhibition site can be seen in the background, the whiteness of the buildings a clear contrast to the otherwise grey and drab vicinity. The stadium was built for the exhibition and was also used for the 1908 Olympic Games. It later became the White City stadium and survived until 1985.

ACKNOWLEDGEMENTS

There are far too many friends and family who over the last 50 years have encouraged and assisted me in collecting my London postcards, which has resulted in this book. As such, those who are not mentioned here, you have not been forgotten in the many, many years of my deltiology.

However, it goes without saying that I must mention my London family and friends who have always been my most loyal and ardent supporters, and have encouraged me to proceed to have this book published on London - my former home of some 35 years, and my favourite city in the world.

My loving sister ShahadhAzam who resides in Harrow, along with my wonderful nieces and nephews – Ayshea, Ahmend, Ali, Faiza and Usman (together with Lydsey, Jumeela and Shahzia, my lovely niece in-laws) have all given me steadfast support in my postcard hunting.

My Brothers Bari and Hamed, and wives Masurat and Karen, plus my nephew Khurram and his wife Maria in LA, and nieces Sofia and Jacki have also never faulted in their belief in my abilities to bring this project to fruition.

My caring "sister"Gurmesh (Carol) Shina and son (Raj) Bobby in Hounslow have been my Rocks since 1979 and my home base in London ever since I retired from British Airways and moved back to Middlesbrough in 2004. London friends Moni and Jaz Gill, Tony Coombes, Laylay Hitchens, Lulu, Waqas Butt and John Monaghan, Peter Vanvacasshave all given me encouragement and support over the years.

Thanks to former London friends now living abroad,Tahiree Mahmood in Houston, Ravi Kakudia in Washington DC and Hamzah Elahi in Islamabad, plus those ex-London residents now living in other parts of the UK such as Coleen Jennings and cousin Robina Asghar. Catherine Powloski, daughter Rosa and son Tyler and the late Mike Powloskiwere never far away in their willingness when I needed their help with transport or accommodation both before and after I lived in London.Cathy a particularly dear friend since 1968 who gave me the key to her London home for me to come and go as I wished during my many, postcard hunting trips in the early 1970s.

Family in Leicester that have always given me their unending support are my very loving cousins Ejaz, Sahahbaz, Imtiaz and Nisa plus niece Maleha in addition to my good friend David Stevens.

Mention must be made of my friends and extensive extended and loving family in Pakistan. They are always very enthusiastic in their support for all my book projects. A very special mention of my caring and loving nephews Rizwan (Rizzy) and Saqlaine Rajpoot, first cousins Irshad, Mushtaq and Ashfaq and their families. Plus Safdar, Ahsan, Ibi, Raza, Shahid, Zahid, Mujaid, Hammad and Shazi and nieces Shahneela, Burrah, Fatima, Masurat, Urooj, Aniba, Laiba, Zainab, Naila, Nuhat, Rahat, Farhat and not forgetting friends Ahmed and Mohammed

Ali - all of whom are from Mcleodganj. Each and every one of them have always thought how wonderful a project this London book and my collection were and their support as always has been second to none.

My other nephews and Nieces in Lahore: Vicky and Furrva, Noor and Menah plus Naveed, Faisal, Lubna and Zawar and cousins RucckkaRaees and Bano. In Gujranwala, my very caring nephew Azam, his brothers and all their families as well as niece Nunee and her family, plus cousins Tipu, his brother and sister Shahzia and all their family Tahira, Zary and Mohammed. Also Hassan, Abu Baker (AB) and Umer. In NowserraVirkan, Zeeshan, Arslan and niece, Rabia, plus cousins Riaz, Zulfikar, Imran and Gulshan – none have wavered in their love and support of myprojects.First and foremost amongst them are close friends Usman Saeed, Esson and Amir, together with Itsham, Kizzer, Shahbir and MianFaisel (of AI-BAIK). Other Cousins and their families are Zubaidah in Singapore plus Nassem, Roshan and niece Azmeena in Malaysia, andMehmoodah, Abbida and Riaz in Melbourne.

My other dearest Australian "family" in Perth are Doris, Glenn, Kim & Kevin and the rest of the wonderful Hankinson Clan who have been my stalwart supporters since we first met on 24 June1982 on the now famous BA009 flight from KL to Perth. Sadly the late DadaKieth Hankinson would have been so very proud of this book as he loved London so much. Two of my most ardent and loyal friends, once residents of Teesside and now in Western Australia, are David and Sandy Smith whom although now thousands of miles away have been in the forefront with their wholehearted support of my endeavours, especially David, my dearest of friends. In New Zealand my "family" are Alex and Rita Eastwood and good friend Betty Tootell, always in my heart as they have never been far away with their help and support. Other"family" are the Timotheuo kinsfolk and particularly my "Feelay&Otherforce" Kyriakos plus good friends Americano and Marilyn in Nicosia, Cyprus. Their Love for London ensures they visit at least once a year and they have been encouraging me and "waiting years"for me to finally complete this book.

Close Middlesbrough friends and family to thank for their interest are Raja Asghar, BajiShumshad, Perveen& Ken Ahmad-Dinsdale and all their family. A special mention to thank my very caring and generous friends Sue Martin and Ron Johnson in addition to my very informative friend Audrey Dewjee from Knaresborough. Not forgetting in Bristol my loving cousins Zehra & Ikram UlHaq plus son Nabeel who have always been supportive of my trips to the West Country with their generous hospitality.

I owe a debt of Great gratitude to my close friend Shaheen Mehdi for inviting me to use the computer facilities in his quite flat to put the finishing touches to this book.

Last but not least and without who's continuing help and total support this book would not have been possible - A very big and special Thank You is owed to Matt Falcus, my Publisher but also my most wonderful friend - Thanks Matt.

Above all is the Love and patience of all my family and friends. My late and loving nephew Harroon who always enjoyed looking at my postcard collection and having been on a trip with me when he was a little younger,the London postcards were his favourite. Also Mr. Colin Bage and the late May Bage.

More than anyone else my late Father and Mother were especially supportive ever since I started collecting postcards way back in 1966 and were always there for me with their encouragement in helping and supporting me at every stage of this very long journey culminating in this, my look at London As It Was.